Aunt Ruth Grammar Drills for Excellence I Answer Key

A Workbook Companion to

I Laid an Egg on Aunt Ruth's Head

by

Joel Schnoor

Gennesaret Press
202 Persimmon Place
Apex, NC 27523

www.gennesaretpress.com

ISBN: 978-0-9845541-9-5

Printed in the United States of America
Apex, North Carolina

Front cover illustration by Doug Oglesby
Interior art by Ken High

Table of Contents

Note: The "From Book Chapter (#)" column below corresponds with the chapter number in *I Laid an Egg on Aunt Ruth's Head* in which that particular topic was discussed.

Lesson 1

Lie and Lay (Part A)

Use forms of lie to complete these sentences.

1. Aunt Ruth, thoroughly exhausted from her adventures, is going to <u>lie</u> down and take a nap!

2. Yesterday, Binky <u>lay</u> down and took a nap.

3. Lois has <u>lain</u> down on the couch recently.

4. I was <u>lying</u> in bed when you called me. I'm telling you the truth!

Use forms of lay or lie to complete the following sentences.

5. I was busy <u>laying</u> the new sod in the back yard. I didn't notice that Aunt Ruth was <u>lying</u> on a blanket, sunning herself. I'll dig her up tomorrow.

6. Last night, the chickens watched in amazement as Clovis <u>laid</u> the book on the shelf.

7. He has no idea what he is doing. He has never <u>laid</u> new carpet.

8. I need to <u>lay</u> the egg on Aunt Ruth's head before she awakens.

Use the appropriate word to complete the sentence.

9. This worksheet is exhausting me. I need to <u>lie</u> down a while and rest.

10. He <u>lay</u> in bed all last week with the flu.

11. It's not polite to <u>lie</u> on the couch when we have guests; you should be sitting!

12. She has <u>lain</u> on the floor all day watching Aunt Ruth exercise!

Lesson 2

Lie and Lay (Part B)

Find the seven errors with lie and lay in the story below; write the corrections. (Correct answers are in parentheses.)

It was a dark and stormy afternoon, and Philbert was **laying**[(lying)] beneath the pecan tree. Next to him was his favorite hen, Rosie, who had **lain**[(laid)] four eggs that very day. I'm not lying.

Now, Philbert had **laid**[(lain)] beneath that tree before, and he had always enjoyed watching the squirrels scurry back and forth on the branches as they gathered nuts for dinner. On this particular afternoon, as he **lied**[(lay)] there with his eyes closed, he was listening to the sounds of the squirrels chattering. Rosie, too, seemed to be enjoying the squirrels as she worked on laying another egg. She had **lay**[(laid)] eggs there before and always enjoyed the furry little critters.

As he lay there, he began drifting off to sleep. He had a dream that a giant squirrel was climbing the tree, in search of the world's largest pecan. He imagined that the branches were creaking, twigs were snapping, and the tree was swaying under the weight of the huge squirrel.

Laying[(Lying)] there, he was startled awake when he heard a clearly audible voice say, "I think I can, I think I can." He opened his eyes. Above him, perched in the tree, was Aunt Ruth! Carrying a bag of nuts and a bottle of glue, she was gluing the pecans onto the tree! Philbert watched her. She would glue a pecan and then eat a pecan; she would glue another pecan, and then she would eat another pecan.

"What are you doing, Aunt Ruth?" exclaimed Philbert. This startled Aunt Ruth, who hadn't seen him as he **laid**[(lay)] there below, and she lost her balance and fell out of the tree, landing right on top of Philbert and Rosie.

"Oh, you caught me," sighed Aunt Ruth. "I'm the Pecan Fairy, going around the world and gluing pecans onto all the pecan trees."

Rosie looked at Aunt Ruth, and then she clucked, "Are you nuts?"

Lesson 3

Hopefully (Part A)

Hint on Hopefully: Note that, in general, if you can substitute "I hope that" for "hopefully," then the "hopefully" is probably being used incorrectly.

Are the following sentences correct?

Example: Hopefully, it will rain tomorrow. <u>No</u>, this is not correct. It does not make sense that "it" will rain in a hopeful manner.

Example: Hopefully, I put a cake in the oven. <u>Yes</u>, this is correct. I was hoping the cake would turn out well when I put it in the oven.

1. N Hopefully, she won't forget about the party. (This is not a correct sentence because it does not really make sense to be hopeful while forgetting or not forgetting something. The sentence makes more sense with this rewriting: I hope that she won't forget about the party.)

2. Y Hopefully, Aunt Ruth stepped into the time machine. (This is correct because when Aunt Ruth stepped into the time machine she was hopeful that she would end up in the right place at the right time.)

3. N Hopefully, the mailman will be on time. (This is not generally correct because why would the mailman be hopeful when he comes on time? Maybe he or she is hopeful about something, but we don't know that from this context.)

4. Y Hopefully, I planned the surprise birthday party. (This is correct because when I planned the party I was hopeful that the surprise would truly be a surprise.)

5. N Hopefully, this lesson on hopefully isn't too confusing. (The lesson cannot really be hopeful about anything.)

6. Y I hopefully auditioned for the symphony. (When I auditioned, I was hopeful that I would be chosen for the symphony.)

Lesson 4

Hopefully (Part B)

Use "Hopefully," or "I hope that" as appropriate.

1. <u>I hope that</u> we will have a good snow this winter.

2. <u>I hope that</u> the meeting will be a success.

3. <u>Hopefully</u>, the little girl planted the carrot seed.

4. <u>Hopefully</u>, I applied for the job.

5. <u>Hopefully</u>, Aunt Ruth invited the nauseating nephew over for dinner (she was hopeful that he will behave himself).

6. <u>I hope that</u> we will have a sunny afternoon for the picnic.

7. <u>I hope that</u> the marching band will perform well. (If the band was hopeful of playing well, we could say, "Hopefully, the marching band performed.")

8. <u>Hopefully</u>, the marching band rehearsed.

Other adverbs can cause similar problems. Are these correct?

1. N Luckily, the frog landed in your soup and not in mine. (The frog did not land in a lucky manner in either soup.)

2. N Importantly, the invitation arrived today. (The invitation did not arrive in an important manner. I suppose it could have, had it been delivered by a royal entourage, but in general this is not how "importantly" would be used.)

3. Y Importantly, the little boy marched down the street with his tuba. The boy marched in a manner displaying importance (or at least he thought he was important).

Lesson 5

Little and Small

Are these sentences correct?

1. N   I am a small hungry this morning.

2. Y   I was a little tired last night.

3. Y   A small bird sat on the window sill.

4. Y   A little bird sat on the window sill.

Use little or small to complete the following sentences. If either will work, write "little / small" in the blank.

5. The papa bear was a <u>little</u> angry at Goldilocks.

6. The man was a <u>little</u> thirsty after being in the desert.

7. Could I have a <u>little</u> of your ice cream please?

8. I would also like a <u>little / small</u> piece of your rhubarb pie, please.

Are these sentences correct?

9. Y   I ate a little toast for breakfast.

10. N   I was a small dismayed this morning when I awoke and found that Binky had eaten my breakfast.

11. Y   I drank a little milk for breakfast.

12. Y   I ate a small piece of toast.

13. N   Can you play the tuba just a small more quietly please?

Lesson 6

Pronouns with To Be

Are these sentences correct?

1. Y   Hello, this is she.

2. N   Hello, this is her.

3. Y   For whom is this gift intended?

4. Y   He thinks he is who?

5. N   Yes, I am him.

6. Y   She gave cookies to Aunt Ruth and me.

7. N   Us gave cookies to her.

8. Y   Those who have blue umbrellas are we.

9. Y   They hoped the blue umbrellas were sent to us.

10. Y   She gave cookies to us.

11. N   She gave cookies to Aunt Ruth and I.

12. N   Aunt Ruth and me gave cookies to her.

Use who or whom to complete the following sentences.

13. You are going to sing to **whom** ?

14. To **whom** are you going to sing ?

15. The next king will be **who** ?

16. **Who** is going to give what to **whom** ?

Lesson 7

Aren't and Comprise

Are these sentences acceptable generally in formal writing wherever English is used?

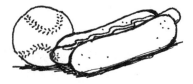

1. Y   I am not the king.

2. N   I amn't the king.

3. N   I are not the king.

4. Y   Aren't I the king?

5. N   I ain't the king!

Are these sentences correct?

1. Y   Our zoo comprises apes and boars.

2. N   The six of us comprise our family.

3. N   Thousands of books comprise a library.

4. Y   The kingdom comprises many people.

5. Y   The ocean comprises many fish.

6. N   Many adventures comprise Aunt Ruth's life.

Lesson 8

Review 1

Are the following sentences correct? (Corrections are in parentheses.)

1. N He gave the possums to they and we. (... to them and us.)

2. N Madge gave the guacamole dip to we. (... to us.)

3. Y Aunt Ruth modeled her new shoes for us and them.

4. N My uncle, Bill Grogan, served Clovis and I a goat dinner. (... and me ...)

5. N Max gave Moby and I two cents each. (... and me ...)

6. N Hopefully, she will bring the gizzards. (I hope that ...)

7. N I laid down for a nap this afternoon. (... lay ...)

8. N Aren't you just a small curious? (... a little curious ...)

9. Y Ask not for whom the phone rings; it rings for thee.

10. N Whom stole the cookies from the jar? (Who stole ...)

11. Y Aunt Ruth's elephant, Binky, is little.

12. N I wanted to be a writer; now I are one. (... I am one ...)

13. Y This test comprises many interesting questions.

14. N Ain't that the greatest thing you have ever heard? (Isn't that ...)

15. Y Aren't I Aunt Ruth's favorite nauseating nephew?

Lesson 9

Can and May

Are these sentences correct (under normal circumstances)?

Example: Can I play violin tonight after dinner? This would not be correct, unless you somehow might have the ability to play after dinner even though you couldn't before dinner.

1. N Can I sit in that chair?

2. Y May I go out to dinner with Hank?

3. Y I can throw a baseball.

4. Y I may throw a baseball outside, but not in the house.

5. Y Mr. Musial, can you hit it over the fence?

6. N Can I walk your dog?

7. Y May I have a piece of that pie?

8. N Can I have a salad?

9. Y Can I go to college next year? (This could reasonably be either **can** or **may**, depending on whether the person was asking about ability or for permission.)

Use may or can to complete the following sentences.

10. No, you **may** not go to the movie tonight.

11. I **can** eat a whole pizza myself.

12. **May** I have the tape measure, please?

13. **May** I go fishing after breakfast?

Lesson 10

Further and Farther

Are these sentences correct?

1. N I need to look into this issue farther.
   (If *farther* is used, it is only for distance.)

2. Y I can throw the ball further than you.

3. Y I am further along with this book.

4. Y For a farthing, my father threw Aunt Ruth's elephant farther.

As and Like

Are the following sentences correct?

1. Y You look as though you saw a lima bean.

2. Y You look like a garbanzo bean.

3. Y You look as though you ate a toad.

4. N You look like you ate a frog. (... as though you ate ...)

5. Y I feel like a koala.

6. N I feel like I have run the gauntlet. (... as though I have run ...)

7. Y Sometimes I feel like a big owl.

8. Y You look as though you don't give a hoot.

9. Y Aunt Ruth waddles like a duck.

10. Y He looked as if he were contemplating something deep

Lesson 11

Review 2

Use who or whom to complete the following sentences.

1. You want to give the broccoli to **whom** ?

2. You are going to sing to **whom** ?

3. To **whom** are you going to sing ?

4. **Who** will be the next king?

5. The next king will be **who** ?

6. **Who** is going to give what to **whom** ?

Are these sentences correct?

7. Y I felt like a million bucks. That's a lot of venison.

8. Y I felt as if I could eat a horse.

9. N I felt like I could eat a horse.

10. Y He eats cereal like a cat that slurps milk from a bowl.

11. Y You look like Albert Einstein on a bad hair day.

12. N It looks like it might rain today.

13. Y It was he who answered the telephone.

14. Y I really think I can do this.

Lesson 12

Review 3

Are these sentences correct? (Corrections are in parentheses.)

1. Y   She gave cookies to Aunt Ruth and me.

2. Y   She gave cookies to us.

3. N   He sold his baseball cards to Loretta and I. (... to Loretta and me.)

4. N   Aunt Ruth and me gave cookies to her. (Aunt Ruth and I ...)

5. N   Us gave cookies to her. (We gave cookies ...)

6. Y   Those who have blue umbrellas are we.

7. Y   They hoped the blue umbrellas were sent to us.

8. N   I gave the apple pie to she. (... to her.)

9. Y   Can I fit into your shoes?

10. N   Can I wear your shoes? (May I wear ...)

11. Y   May I eat your salad?

12. Y   Hopefully, I submitted the manuscript to the publisher.

Use lie or lay (or forms thereof) to complete the following sentences.

13. I **laid** my coat on the table this morning.

14. I need to **lay** my book on the counter for a moment.

15. Yesterday, he **lay** down to catch up on rest.

Lesson 13

That and Which

Fill in the blank with the correct word, that or which.

1. The spider **that** sat down beside her was friendly and jovial.

2. The tuba, **which** is my favorite instrument, can lull a hound dog to sleep and send a cat into hysterics at the same time.

3. This is the day **that** the Lord has made. Let us rejoice and be glad!

4. The persimmon **that** is on the counter is yours.

5. The persimmon, **which** is a most unusual fruit, is gaining popularity.

6. The thing **that** has twenty-two legs is crawling up your back.

7. People worry about too many things, but there are few things **that** really matter.

8. Her favorite song, **which** is also one of my favorites, is by Beethoven.

9. **Which** board game do you think is the best?

10. Was this the face **that** launched a thousand ships and burnt the topless towers of Ilium?

11. **That** was one of the happiest moments of my life!

12. I am really enjoying the book **that** you gave me.

13. What is the favorite thing **that** you did last summer?

14. Would you rather eat a bowl of ice cream or do these worksheets **that** I gave you?

Lesson 14

If I Were

Are these sentences correct?

1. Y   If I were not the king, I would not have told them to eat cake.

2. Y   Well, if I were just a bit taller, I wouldn't fit in my skin.

3. Y   You say that you saw me in a blue sweatshirt? If I was there, I'd have worn my red sweatshirt. (Hint: I was there.)

4. Y   If I were you, I'd eat the bratwurst and then the sauerkraut, instead of the other way around. (I can never be you, but this is a hypothetical case.)

5. Y   If I were to rob a bank, I certainly wouldn't go about it the way that he did.

6. N   If I was just a little bit older, I would certainly feel younger than I am. (I am not a little bit older, so this is false; use **were**.)

7. N   If Jeremiah was a kangaroo instead of a bullfrog, do you think he would still be a really good friend of yours?

8. N   If I was an astronaut with a spaceship, just think of all the cool places I could go!

9. Y   If I were the king of my own little country, I would declare every day to be a grammar holiday.

10. Y   My boss was Mr. Ware. I always said that if my boss was Ware, then that meant I was working under Ware.

Lesson 15

Verbing or Verbizing

Verbing or verbizing is taking a noun and turning it into a verb. Many words used today were formed that way. For example, we used to give or receive gifts. Now we can **gift** something. We can even re-gift it, if we care. The following verbs were all created from nouns originally.

Hospitalizing, Utilizing, Onboarding, Computerizing, Landscaping

Can you come up with some on your own (even silly sounding words are fine, such as tuba-ize)? Here are some examples for your inspiration.

Pepperize (perhaps adding pepper to a meal)
Volumize (perhaps increasing the loudness of music)
Decalorize (perhaps burning calories while exercising)

Circle all the non-words you find below. (Answers are underlined here.)

Henry was cooking breakfast when his roommate walked in.
"Hi Henry," said George. "What are you doing?"
"I am **omeletting** some eggs."
"Mmm. Would you mind **omeletting** one for me too?"
"No problem. Are you going to do some **magazining** this morning?"
"No, I **magazined** last night. I think I'll **piano-ize** for a while."
"So are you going to **Chopinize** or **Beethovenize** today?"
"I think I'll do some **Gershwining**, actually."
"Oh, your **Gershwining** is so good ... are you thinking of Rhapsody in **Blueing**?"
"I thought I might **Prelude-ize**."
"Hey, I'm going to go **orchardize** some apples later this morning. They're ripe now."
"Well, if you **orchardize**, I'll be happy to **pie-ize** this afternoon."
"Oh man, ice **creamizing** a hot apple pie would be perfect."
"Oh I love **dessertizing**!"
"What are you going to **breakfastize** tomorrow?
"I'm waffling." (Waffling is a real word.)

Lesson 16

Anybody and Everybody

Are the following sentences correct?

1. Y Everybody has to do his homework before tomorrow.

2. N Anybody who wants to can stand up from their seat. (... his seat.)

3. N None of us have ever gone to Mars, except for Aunt Ruth. (None of us has ...)

4. N If someone wants to, they can go get food for the rest of us. (... he can go ...)

5. Y All of them are crazy!

6. Y Every writer has his or her sources of inspiration.

7. N Everyone thinks they should be first in line. (... he or she ...)

8. Y Nobody says he thinks that Binky should be president.

9. N None of them are going to the zoo to see Aunt Ruth. (... None of them is ...)

10. N Nobody should skip their breakfast! (... his or her breakfast!)

11. Y Nobody should skip his or her breakfast.

12. N If anyone thinks Binky is tiny, they're crazy. (... he or she is crazy.)

13. Y Everybody who has met Aunt Ruth will never forget her.

14. Y Everyone is going to have to tie his shoes before leaving the room.

15. Y Each of the students has to do his or her own homework.

16. N No one has to do their taxes this year. (... his taxes ...)

17. N Nobody knows their pets better than Noah. (... his pets better ...)

Lesson 17

Will and Shall

Circle will or shall as appropriate. In cases where either will work, circle both.

1. It's hard to believe that you **will** be seventeen tomorrow!

2. I **will / shall** go to the ballgame tonight.

3. He **will** be going to the restaurant this weekend.

4. You **shall** pay homage to me, the king.

5. She **will** be working this Saturday.

6. She **shall** lead this team, or else I will fire her.

7. I **will / shall** be there for breakfast in the morning.

8. You **will** be there too, right?

9. **Will** he be there also?

10. I **will** make it through the mountains, or else!

11. We **will / shall** be going to the play together!

12. Barney was thirsty, so he drew water from the **well**.

13. **Will** Rogers said he never met a man he didn't like.

14. When I die, my **will** specifies that each of my children will receive a copy of *I Laid an Egg on Aunt Ruth's Head* (autographed, of course).

15. You **shall** pay the rent, or I will evict you!

16. I am determined that I **will** not pay the rent until you take the elephant away.

Lesson 18

It's and Its

Are these sentences correct?

1. N Its about time you invited Aunt Ruth over to your house, don't you think?

2. N Many thought Gerald wanted to escape, but for a content goldfish, escaping was the furthest thing from it's mind.

3. Y I saw a red fox this morning. Its tail was so pretty.

4. Y We have had the family car for ten years now, and I think it's on its last legs.

Fill in the blank with the correct word, either its or it's.

5. It looks like __it's__ going to be a long day at the park with Aunt Ruth.

6. I found our chicken busily laying __its__ eggs on Aunt Ruth's head.

7. Have you ever seen Saturn through a telescope? __Its__ rings are simply beautiful.

8. __It's__ time for lunch! I wonder what Aunt Ruth will stir up in her cauldron.

9. How much is the elephant in the window? Yes, I mean the one with __its__ ears cut short and __its__ tail cut long.

Are these sentences correct?

10. Y It's simply amazing!
11. N Its another day at the office.
12. Y Its back is scaly and its scalp is furry.
13. Y It's time for Aunt Ruth's birthday celebration.
14. Y It's its tenth time that it's taken food from our bird feeder today!

Lesson 19

Review 4

Select the appropriate words.

1. He **lay** in bed all last week with the flu.

2. She had **lain** in bed all last week with pneumonia.

3. **Hopefully** she hung the laundry outside to dry.

4. **I hope that** the wolf will not get the three little pigs this time.

5. She gave an elephant to Clovis and **me**.

6. To **whom** are you going to sing?

7. **May** we throw a baseball around after dinner?

8. The committee needs to look at the bill a little **further**.

9. If I **were** Charlie Chaplin, I would have spoken up better in those movies.

10. Everybody **has** at least two chickens.

11. None of us **needs** to eat dessert at the restaurant tonight.

12. Is it true that you **will** be playing the tuba next week?

13. **It's** going to be a long afternoon for the penguin and **its** pet iguana.

14. **May** I be excused from this worksheet so I can get back to my writing?

15. I **laid** the book aside somewhere and now I cannot find it.

16. I was **lying** down on the couch when Aunt Ruth threw the javelin through the window.

Lesson 20

Parentheses

Correct the punctuation in all sentences found below, keeping all parentheses. If the sentence is already correct, write Correct.

1. Some people can be delightful (like Aunt Ruth.).
   Some people can be delightful (like Aunt Ruth).

2. Some people can be obstreperously stubborn (like Aunt Ruth.)
   Some people can be obstreperously stubborn (like Aunt Ruth).

3. (A standalone sentence such as this can have the punctuation inside the parentheses.)
   Correct

4. A sentence such as this needs to have the punctuation outside the parentheses (such as this).
   Correct

5. Remember, you need to be able to remove the entire parenthetical expression without damaging the rest of the sentence, (and this sentence would break).
   Remember, you need to be able to remove the entire parenthetical expression without damaging the rest of the sentence (and this sentence would break).

6. These worksheets are the greatest thing ever (next to traveling to sixteenth century Italy with Aunt Ruth, that is).
   Correct

7. When I see parentheses, I feel the need to (quietly) whisper (like this.).
   When I see parentheses, I feel the need to (quietly) whisper (like this).

8. Some sentences have too many parentheses (but don't you just love these things?).
   Correct

Lesson 21

Lose and Loose

It seems that when most people get this wrong, it is because they use "loose" when they should use "lose."

Use lose or loose as appropriate.

1. I hope I don't <u>lose</u> my mind before the day is done.

2. I'm thin now and my pants are too <u>loose</u>.

3. I hope Aunt Ruth doesn't <u>lose</u> her elephant Binky.

4. Aunt Ruth rarely wears clothes that are too <u>loose</u>.

5. It's possible to play hard and still <u>lose</u> the ballgame.

6. Attention! The iguana is on the <u>loose</u>.

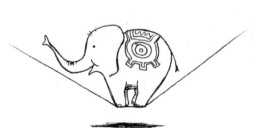

7. I <u>lose</u> my car keys frequently.

8. My shoestrings are usually too <u>loose</u>.

9. Do you get mad when you <u>lose</u> a friendly game?

10. Don't let the dog <u>loose</u> from his leash or you might <u>lose</u> him.

11. We are ahead with only two minutes left. I hope we don't <u>lose</u>.

12. Stay calm. Don't <u>lose</u> your composure.

13. Keep your autographed picture of Aunt Ruth. You don't want to <u>lose</u> that.

14. Hey, who let Aunt Ruth <u>loose</u> from her cage?

Lesson 22

Well and Good

Name 3 things that make you feel good (e.g., reading a book on a rainy day):

1. __(student's choice)_____

2. _____

3. _____

Name 3 things that you want to do well (e.g., play the tuba):

1. __(student's choice)_____

2. _____

3. _____

Circle the best answers.

a. You are helping an old lady across the street. You are **doing good** / doing well.

b. You wake up feeling cheerful, happy, and smiling. Someone asks you how you are. You say: I am well / **I am good**.

c. Someone asks you how you are doing. You say: **I am well** / I am good. (The "doing" is implied, as in, "I am doing well." Either response is acceptable, though.)

d. You have been sick all week, and finally you start to feel better. Someone asks how you feel. You say: **I feel well** / I feel good.

e. Your hands have poor circulation and the cold weather has made your fingers numb. How do you feel? **Not well** / Not good.

f. You see a Santa Claus at the mall. He asks you if you have been good or bad. You say: **I have been good** / I have been well.

Lesson 23

Apostrophes

Circle the 29 apostrophe errors in the story below.

Aunt Ruth once had a pet iguana named Elmer. Now, Elmer had been <u>her's</u> for several <u>year's</u>, and during that time Elmer had developed some odd <u>habit's</u>.

<u>It's</u> first interesting habit occurred each day when it would go out and get the two morning <u>newspaper's</u>. That <u>wasnt</u> the odd part. The odd part was that Elmer would sing the <u>newspapers</u> contents loudly on the street corner, accompanied by his little electric guitar. Its singing <u>wasnt</u> bad for an iguana, and <u>it's</u> guitar playing was pretty good. Elmer's rendition of Iguana Hold Your Hand made the Top 40 Reptile <u>Hit's</u>, second only to a version of Godzilla as performed by the Purple Mussel <u>Followers'</u>.

Its second quirk was that it would only take <u>it's</u> <u>bath's</u> each night at midnight, and <u>it's</u> preferred water temperature was ice cold. Aunt Ruth would diligently scrub <u>it's</u> back and under its arms, and then she would brush its teeth. Elmer was also good about having <u>it's</u> teeth flossed.

<u>Elmers</u> skin had bright <u>color's</u>, especially in the sunshine. The <u>blue's</u>, <u>silver's</u>, <u>green's</u>, and sometimes even the <u>red's</u> would show off nicely. <u>Elmers</u> photographs appealed to many advertising <u>agent's</u>, and Elmer received offers from some of Madison Avenues biggest <u>name's</u>.

The iguana loved New York City, but he missed Aunt Ruth and her wacky adventures. Occasionally, Aunt Ruth's mailbox would contain a letter from Elmer, and this always delighted her. Then, on one fine spring afternoon, Aunt Ruth opened her mailbox and was surprised to see Elmer standing inside, smiling at her.

They hugged and danced, and then they went out and ate a couple of <u>pizza's</u>.

Elmer went to nearby Iguana University and became a writer of grammar <u>book's</u>. Elmer kept in touch with Aunt Ruth—in fact, for years they had breakfast together on <u>Saturday's</u>—and <u>Elmers</u> life was filled with happiness for ever after.

Lesson 24

Real and Really

Are these sentences correct? (Corrections in parentheses.)

1. N I saw a real good movie.   (I saw a **really** good movie.)

2. Y He's a really interesting person.

3. Y The loss was a real blow for morale.

4. Y Yes, I really am going to invite Aunt Ruth over for dinner.

5. N When I go fishing, I like to use a rod and real. (I like to use a rod and **reel**.)

6. N It was a real dark and stormy night. (It was a **really** dark and stormy night.)

7. Y That's a really great book.

Find the four errors in the story below. (Answers are underlined.)

Bobbi had a <u>real</u> good time at the state fair. First, she bought some cotton candy, made from real maple syrup. It was really cheap, so she bought a lot of it (and ate it all). Then she bought some peanuts, and they were really good.

While walking through the Midway, Bobbi saw something really shocking—life-sized chocolate elephants. She was not really hungry, so she only bought one chocolate elephant. It weighed 300 pounds—really heavy! Bobbi sat down and ate the <u>real</u> big chocolate elephant fairly quickly, finishing in about 15 minutes. When she finished, she felt so full, and she began to worry. She was <u>real</u> concerned because she had eaten so much that she thought she would explode.

At that moment, someone accidentally dropped a candied apple from the ferris wheel, and it landed on top of Bobbi's head. The people in the crowd held their breaths a long time; they were really worried that Bobbi would pop. She didn't though, and the crowd was <u>real</u> happy.

Bobbi never really ate that much bad food again, ever. That's the real truth.

Lesson 25

There, They're, and Their

Find the fourteen incorrect uses of there, their, or they're in the story below.

<u>Their</u> once was a dog who had a pet boy, and they liked to spend **<u>they're</u>** time out in the woods. On one of **<u>there</u>** outings, the boy saw two cats. He said, "Look Fido, those cats are fishing, but **<u>their</u>** using **<u>there</u>** fishing poles instead of **<u>they're</u>** claws. They don't have any bait on **<u>they're</u>** hooks"

Fido looked at the cats and **<u>they're</u>** fishing poles.

The cats looked at Fido and the boy and noticed that they were staring at their fishing poles. They didn't like people staring at their fishing poles, but they decided it would be in their best interest if they continued their fishing.

Then the boy said, "Should we go help them with **<u>there</u>** fishing?"

Fido smiled and wiggled his ears.

The boy said, "Okay, come with me. We'll show them how to put bait on the hooks. They'll need to know that if **<u>their</u>** going to catch any fish."

Fido smiled at the boy and said, "You're right! I think they're going to need to learn how to fish."

The boy looked at Fido and said, "Hey wait, you can talk!"

Fido looked at the boy and said, "**<u>Their</u>, <u>their</u>**, don't be too surprised. We're just characters in a story, remember?"

After the dog and his pet boy helped teach the cats how to fish, they walked back to **<u>they're</u>** house, where they spent the rest of **<u>there</u>** days living happily ever after.

Lesson 26

Your, You're, and Yours

Are these sentences correct?

1. N   Your the apple of my eye. (You're)

2. N   I think this is you're dog. (your)

3. Y   What is your cat doing here?

4. Y   You're so funny!

5. Y   This is yours, not mine.

6. N   How did you spend you're evening? (your)

7. N   Your not serious, are you? (You're)

8. N   <u>Your</u> not sure where your going until you get in <u>you're</u> car and drive a while. (You're, your)

9. N   I believe this is you're possum sandwich. (your)

10. N   Aunt Ruth? No, she's not my aunt. She's your's. (yours)

11. N   I hope your kidding! (you're)

12. N   I thought you said you're dog didn't bite. (your)

13. N   This is you're book, is it not? (your)

14. Y   You're acting a bit goofy this morning.

15. Y   Why, I do believe that these are yours.

16. N   Wait, your kidding, right? (you're)

Lesson 27

Myriad, Complimentary, and Stationery

Find all four incorrect words in the story below.

The boy and his father were out walking in the fields in the middle of October. Even though it was the middle of the day, the sky suddenly became dark. "Look," the boy exclaimed, "the cattle are all migrating south for the winter."

Sure enough, the father looked up only to see myriad cattle flying south. The father **complemented** his son, saying, "Son, you sure have good eyes."

The boy remained **stationery** while the father pulled out his best **stationary** and wrote a letter home, telling his wife about this event. It wasn't all that common to see a myriad of cattle flying south in broad daylight (usually they do their flying at night). In fact, some people still believed that the story of the cow jumping over the moon was only a myth.

One of the cows, a chocolate Guernsey, spotted the boy and his father below, and he diverted his path and landed right in front of them. He bowed low, greeted them with a friendly "moo," and held out a gallon jug of ice cold chocolate milk.

"Thank you," said the father, "but we haven't any money with us. We have no way of paying for chocolate milk."

"Oh, no problem," said the cow. "This is **complementary**."

"Well thanks," said the father. With that, the cow curtsied and took off to catch up with the myriad cattle flying south for the winter.

At that moment, the jug of chocolate milk spoke. "Say there, I like those boots you're wearing, boy. And Mister, that's a mighty fine hat you are wearing, if I do say so myself."

"Thank you," said the polite son. He turned to his father and said, "Dad, the cow was right. This milk really is complimentary!"

Lesson 28

Irregardless and Other Non-Words

Find the twenty non-words (including repeats) in the story below.

Ms. Wigglethorpe was standing in the aisle at the local grocer, trying to decide whether to get the flammable or inflammable hair spray. She was in a quandary, struggling with the decision. **Irregardless** of what she would decide, she felt it was a lose-lose situation. If she opted for the flammable, it might go up in flames. If she opted for the inflammable, it too might end up in flames. Either way could be not fun.

From the back corner of the store, a man emerged wearing a black suit made from lamb's wool. It was a new fashion they call a **baaxedo**. The man spoke.

"**Enpicture** if you will a certain Mrs Wigglethorpe, who was **conflubbulated** while trying to make an **inshopillent** decision. Little did she realize that she had become **superenzoned** ... in the Hair Spray Enigma."

Much to her annoyment, when she orientated herself back toward the front window of the store, she noticed that there was quite a big storm coming. She did some quick analyzation and decided that the inclimate weather would be okay, even though her hair might get wet.

Mrs. Wigglethorpe stared at the man—she was quite the **staremeister**—but then she broke into a fit of **laughication** when she realized he was wearing a **baaxedo**.

"Why, you are wearing a **baaxedo**!" she exclaimed. "You may not have **awareized** it, but I am the designer of the **baaxedo**. It is the centerpiece of my magnificent new line of clothing, **baaxiwear**."

"You invented **baaxiwear**?" the man asked **inquiriously**.

"**Yesdeed**," she smiled, with great cheek **liftication**. "Soon, you will even be able to purchase our new line of male undergarments."

"Oh?" he asked, in a most **querisitive** manner. "What will they be called?"

"**Baaxer** shorts," she said with a **jovialacious** laugh.

Lesson 29

Review 5

Select the appropriate words.

1. I'm not sure how this happens, but Aunt Ruth seems to consistently loose / <u>lose</u> her pet elephant Binky.

2. The night was real / <u>really</u> awful. Binky fell on me while attempting a cart-wheel.

3. So, my head hurt and I just wasn't feeling very <u>well</u> / good when I woke up this morning.

4. "Say, that's a nice tie your / <u>you're</u> wearing," said Binky, who was more complementary / <u>complimentary</u> than the average elephant.

5. Where do elephants keep luggage? In they're / there / <u>their</u> trunks, of course.

6. Binky did not move all day. He was quite <u>stationary</u> / stationery.

7. With a pencil, the little girl wrote a letter on Binky's side. She must have thought Binky was stationary / <u>stationery</u>.

8. Their / <u>They're</u> going to the zoo tomorrow, where they hope to see myriad of / <u>myriad</u> animals.

9. Your / <u>You're</u> certain that those are <u>your</u> / you're plans for the afternoon?

10. <u>Regardless</u> / Irregardless, I hope you show up at the restaurant.

Rewrite the following sentences to use punctuation for parentheses correctly.

11. Binky loves jazz music (his favorite artist is Elephant Gerald.)
    Binky loves jazz music (his favorite artist is Elephant Gerald).

12. Binky can use his trunk to play notes higher than any jazz trumpeter, (except for Maynard Ferguson). (Remove the comma.)

Lesson 30

Capitalization

Find the thirteen capitalization errors.

1. Raleigh is the capital of North Carolina and should be capitalized. I think that <u>richmond</u>, as the capital of Virginia, should be capitalized too.

2. I went to see Professor Aunt Ruth about the test she had given us yesterday. The <u>**Professor**</u> was in a jolly mood and she said that she would give me an A. I said this to her: "I have a question for you, <u>**professor**</u>. Should I capitalize the word professor or not?"

3. She said, "It depends."

4. I had a dream that I met the mayor, the governor, and the president. None of them looked capitalized in the dream. Should they be capitalized in real life? The mayor, Mayor Smith, should have the first word capitalized when it's used with the name or when he/she is being directly addressed. The mayor is funny. You, Mayor, are funny.

5. Of course, names such as Max, George, and <u>**benjamin**</u> need to be capitalized. Titles such as Dr., Mrs., and <u>mr</u>. should be capitalized too.

6. People tend to capitalize words that seem important, but they shouldn't be capitalized. The chief <u>**Topic**</u> for today is <u>**Capitalization**</u>.

7. The Grand Canyon is beautiful, or so I have heard. I have not seen it. I hope to <u>**See**</u> it someday!

8. I wonder if the president wants to take this test? Hello, President, would you like to do these worksheets?

9. I think this is a <u>**Capital Idea**</u>!

10. Many states in the United States have changed their <u>**Capitals**</u> over the years.

11. One does not receive <u>**Capital Punishment**</u> for missing capital letters.

Lesson 31

Split Infinitives

Find the split infinitives (there should be thirteen).

The town came to a standstill as the stranger rode into town on horseback. A chill swept the air; a tumbleweed blew down the street, getting caught on a wagon wheel in front of the barber shop; and a tuba was heard, playing a Bach fugue softly in the background.

The stranger adjusted his cowboy hat and walked into the saloon.

1. "I would like a banana split infinitive please."

2. "Would you like that **to enjoyably eat** here or **to quickly go**?"

3. "Oh, you like **to really confuse** me, don't you!"

4. "I tend **to quite enjoy** that, yes."

5. "Well then, I'd like **to really have** my banana split infinitive here."

6. "Are you going **to additionally order** anything else?"

7. "You mean like whipped cream, a maraschino cherry, and perhaps some chocolate syrup **to ravenously devour**?"

8. "I had wanted **to sarcastically ask** you if you wanted a diet soda with that, but I should decline the temptation **to rudely bother** you with that question."

9. "That's so kind of you. You are a gentleman seeking **to pleasantly help** the customers around you **to thoroughly enjoy** their desserts."

10. "Say, you're not from around here, are you?"

11. "Well no, but I've got **to thankfully tip** my hat to you ... these banana split infinitives are so good I want **to quickly inhale** another one!"

Dangling Participles

Fix the dangling participles and misplaced modifiers below.
Answers will vary.

Example: Flying high overhead, Vic saw the ducks from his hidden duck blind.

(Fixed):   From behind his duck blind, Vic saw the ducks flying high overhead.

1. Raining heavily—in fact, it was an absolutely torrential downpour—I made it from my car to the house without getting too wet.

    In the heavy rain—in fact, it was an absolutely torrential downpour—I made it from my car to the house without getting too wet.

2. Spicier than I normally like, I ate the whole plate of Mexican food that was placed in front of me.

    Even though the Mexican food was spicier than I normally like, I ate the whole plate of food that was placed in front of me.

3. Barking all night long, I was kept awake by the dogs across the street.

    The dogs across the street, barking all night long, kept me awake.

4. Spiraling through the air, I made the perfect pass for the winning touchdown in the football game.

    The ball spiraling through the air, I made the perfect pass for the winning touchdown in the football game.

5. Cheesy and bubbling and piping hot, I love eating macaroni and cheese on a cold autumn day.

    I love eating macaroni and cheese—cheesy and bubbling and piping hot—on a cold autumn day.

Lesson 33

Whoever and Whomever

Select whoever or whomever.

1. You can be **whoever** / whomever you want to be when you grow up.

2. I will give the chocolate covered raisins to **whoever** / whomever wants them.

3. This ticket is for **whoever** / whomever wants to go to the game.

4. The football flew through the air and decided to land on whoever / **whomever** it pleased.

5. The phone is ringing for **whoever** / whomever wants to answer it.

6. The roses on the table are for whoever / **whomever**.

7. Aunt Ruth is saving the fruitcake for whoever / **whomever** she wants to have it—she made it seventeen years ago.

8. The bell will toll for whoever / **whomever** it wants to toll.

9. **Whoever** / Whomever wants to eat now, the food is ready!

10. **Whoever** / Whomever said it is a small world?

11. To whoever / **whomever** it may concern ...

12. Someone took my tooth brush by accident! I hope that **whoever** / whomever has it will not be crestfallen.

13. To **whoever** / whomever it was who borrowed my aardvark, I do wish you would return it.

14. To whoever / **whomever** she gave the fruitcake, she also gave an indelible and inedible memory.

Lesson 34

Using Past Participles

Select the correct word.

Aunt Ruth decided, one fine summer day, to go for a swim.

1. A goose who **swam** / swum every day in the pond was already there.

2. Aunt Ruth saw the goose and **swam** / swum toward it.

3. The goose **swam** / swum across the pond, trying to get away from Aunt Ruth.

4. Aunt Ruth has swam / **swum** after this particular goose before, trying to have it over for dinner.

5. If Aunt Ruth had swam / **swum** faster, she may have caught the goose.

6. The dinner bell had rang / **rung**, and the goose thought this was a warning signal to be on the lookout for Aunt Ruth.

7. The dinner bell **rang** / rung yesterday, too.

8. Aunt Ruth was not intending to eat the goose; if Aunt Ruth had brung / **brought** an invitation before, the goose would have realized that Aunt Ruth wanted to have it over for dinner as a guest, not as the main course.

9. Aunt Ruth brang / **brought** an invitation this time, but the goose refused to get close enough to read it.

10. After the goose swam across the lake, he **ran** / run. After he had ran / **run** a ways, he finally was too tired to run further. Aunt Ruth caught him and invited him for dinner. He was delighted.

What a silly language. What a silly goose!

Lesson 35

Many and Much

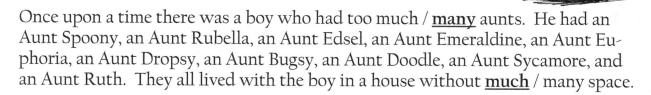

Where given a choice, select the correct word.

Once upon a time there was a boy who had too much / **many** aunts. He had an Aunt Spoony, an Aunt Rubella, an Aunt Edsel, an Aunt Emeraldine, an Aunt Euphoria, an Aunt Dropsy, an Aunt Bugsy, an Aunt Doodle, an Aunt Sycamore, and an Aunt Ruth. They all lived with the boy in a house without **much** / many space.

Believe it or not, on his birthday he complained because he received too much / **many** birthday presents from his aunts. They gave him too much / **many** building blocks, too **much** / many writing paper, too **much** / many birthday cake with too much / **many** candles, too much / **many** books, and too **much** / many milk. He simply did not have room for all of it—he had too **much** / many stuff!

Then it came to pass that the boy grew older—in fact, he grew **much** / many older, and after much / **many** years he ended up older than the aunts. How did that happen? I don't know. But the fact is that he was older than his aunts, and this gave him **much** / many delight.

Now, when it was his much / **many** aunts' birthdays, he would give them some of the much / **many** things that they had given him over the years.

For a while, there was **much** / many complaining by the aunts. After all, they didn't have **much** / many space to put their stuff either. They had too much / **many** things! It was just too **much** / many stuff.

For much / **many** days, the much / **many** aunts sat on the front porch in their much / **many** rocking chairs, pondering what to do. They all agreed with **much** / many enthusiasm that something needed to be done, but they couldn't figure out what to do. There were so much / **many** options. It was **much** / many too confusing.

Then, Aunt Ruth had a great idea. "Let's sell **much** / many of this stuff, getting rid of much / **many** things. We can then give the money to people who need it more than we do."

There was **much** / many rejoicing at this idea, and they all lived much / **many** happy years together in that house.

Lesson 36

Between, Among, Next, This

Select the correct word.

1. **Between** / Among the five of us, we
   should be able to select who's going to take
   Aunt Ruth to the movies.[1]

2. **Between** / Among the two of us, we should be able
   to select who's going to take Aunt Ruth shopping.

3. **Between** / Among you and me, we should be able to select who's going to go
   skydiving with Aunt Ruth.

4. Aunt Ruth and her parachute landed between / **among** the trees in the forest.

5. On her next jump, Aunt Ruth landed **between** / among your house, Elmer's
   house, and my house.

6. **Between** / Among the six of us, we were able to collect enough money to buy
   Aunt Ruth a diet soda.

7. Let's meet at the restaurant **between** / among 7:30 and 7:45 tomorrow night.

8. Choose a number **between** / among one and ten.

9. If today is Tuesday, then this / **next** Wednesday is a week from tomorrow.

10. If today is Tuesday, then **this** / next Wednesday is tomorrow.

11. **This** / Next Thursday is the matinée. Today is Monday. The matinée is three
    days away.

---

1   (Though there are more than two, the group is united in a common cause or objective and
"Between" is better than "Among" here. See the chapter "Common Rough Spots in English" in
the book *I Laid an Egg on Aunt Ruth's Head*.)

Lesson 37

Principle, Principal, Accept, Except

Select the correct word.

1. The book *I Laid an Egg on Aunt Ruth's Head* is based on some of the fundamental principals / <u>**principles**</u> of grammar.

2. I think that the <u>**principal**</u> / principle of each school should make the book required reading for all the students.

3. When will people <u>**accept**</u> / except the responsibility to speak correctly?

4. Everyone took his animal to the pet show, accept / <u>**except**</u> for Aunt Ruth. She had a tough time getting Binky in the car.

5. I just cannot <u>**accept**</u> / except the fact that Binky won't play with me.

6. Accept / <u>**Except**</u> for Thursday night, I'm busy every night this week.

7. I went to the bank to pay off the <u>**principal**</u> / principle amount of the loan.

8. They would not <u>**accept**</u> / except my cash. They said they would only <u>**accept**</u> / except books about Aunt Ruth instead.

9. I was at the ceremony to <u>**accept**</u> / except the award for Aunt Ruth, who somehow had found herself glued to the ceiling of her apartment and was unable to come.

10. The martian invasion was the scariest thing I had ever experienced, accept / <u>**except**</u> for the first time I met Aunt Ruth.

11. This organization has certain <u>**principles**</u> / principals, or guidelines, that we must follow if we are to be successful.

Lesson 38

Review 6

Select the appropriate words.

1. I think whomever / **whoever** wants it can have it.

2. Take this grilled cheese sandwich and give it to **whomever** / whoever.

3. I have swam / **swum** in that pond.

4. The bell had rang / **rung** last month.

5. There is not **much** / many sand, but there are **many** / much grains of sand.

6. **Between** / Among the two of us, I think that soda is overrated.

7. Can you **accept** / except that the principals / **principles** of grammar are important to Aunt Ruth?

Find the capitalization errors in this paragraph.

  the day **i** went to see **The President**, **He** was golfing on the **Front Lawn**. He asked me how I was. I told him I was fine, and then I said, "Mr. President, do you want to have lunch with me?" He thought that was a **Grand Idea**, so we went to Aunt **ruth's** new restaurant. Binky was the **chef**.

Find the split infinitives in this paragraph.

  To courageously fight for what one believes in is important; **to bravely stand** up for one's ideals, however, is not **to brashly say** that we shouldn't be tolerant of others. They have the right **to likewise defend** their beliefs.

Rewrite the sentence below to fix the dangling participle.

  Rising high into the deep blue sky, I noticed the sun on this beautiful day. I noticed the sun, rising high into the deep blue sky, on this beautiful day.

Lesson 39

Wake, Awake, e.g., i.e.

Select the correct word.

1. Aunt Ruth needs to <u>wake</u> / awake up or she will miss the waffles that Binky is making for breakfast.

2. Aunt Ruth was <u>awakened</u> / wokened when there was a raven knocking on her door.

3. Aunt Ruth <u>woke</u> / waked up when Bill the Grammar Fairy came and played the tuba in her room.

4. She <u>awoke</u> / awokened when the bulldozer accidentally knocked down her bedroom wall.

5. After she woke up, Aunt Ruth prepared some of her favorite food, <u>e.g.</u> / E.I.E.I.O., buttermilk pancakes.

6. My favorite color, <u>i.e.</u> / e.g., blue, is in the United States flag.

7. I plan to study Industrial Engineering as my major when I go to college, <u>i.e.</u> / e.g., I.E.

8. I tend to enjoy listening to brass instruments (<u>e.g.</u> / i.e., tuba) more than woodwinds or strings.

9. Aunt Ruth was <u>wakened</u> / wokened by the sounds of a tuba quartet serenading her on her front lawn.

10. I <u>awoke</u> / awoked when Aunt Ruth knocked on my door at 2 a.m.

11. Some pieces of literature, i.e. / <u>e.g.</u>, *I Laid an Egg on Aunt Ruth's Head*, are simply magnificent works of art.

Lesson 40

Dessert, Desert

Select the correct word.

1. My favorite deserts / <u>desserts</u> all have chocolate in them.

2. I <u>figuratively</u> / literally felt as though I were about a zillion years old this morning when I woke up.

3. Can you <u>ensure</u> / insure that Aunt Ruth never gives me another fruit cake?

4. The Sahara <u>desert</u> / dessert is one of the most impressive in all the world.

5. I figuratively / <u>literally</u> forgot where I was supposed to be last night.

6. You should ensure / <u>insure</u> your tuba against possible theft or damage.

7. May we have some desert / <u>dessert</u> after dinner tonight?

8. He <u>figuratively</u> / literally can throw the ball a million miles an hour.

9. Well son, I want you to <u>ensure</u> / insure that it never happens again.

10. I've <u>figuratively</u> / literally told you a billion times that you need to clean your plate off if you expect to get any desert / <u>dessert</u>.

11. I'm so glad my car was ensured / <u>insured</u>! Who would have expected someone to drop one of Aunt Ruth's fruitcakes from a bridge onto my car?

12. Waiter, there's a camel in my desert / <u>dessert</u>.

13. Surrounded by billions upon billions of grains of sand, Lawrence saw it. There, on top of a mound of sand, was a maraschino cherry. "Somebody," he thought to himself, "has made a big mistake. This place is a <u>desert</u> / dessert."

Lesson 41

Alright and All Right

Select the correct word.

1. Alright / **All right** folks, it's time to get this show on the road.

2. Hey dude, I hope you are feeling alright / **all right**.

3. I like this book **a lot** / alot.

4. **A lot** / Alot of people are coming to see Aunt Ruth go bungee jumping.

Rewrite each sentence so that it is correct.

5. This fruitcake from 1969 needs eaten.
   This fruitcake from 1969 needs to be eaten.

6. Your cat needs washed.
   Your cat needs to be washed.

7. Your teeth need brushed.
   Your teeth need to be brushed.

Lesson 42

Apostrophes in Names

Find the seventeen errors.

<u>Rubys'</u> dog was a very strange animal. Its name was Rover, but that's not why it was strange. It was strange because it could speak English.

<u>Rovers</u> favorite thing to do on a sunny Saturday afternoon was to go to the park and swing on the swing set. There, Rover would see the Jones family with their 17 <u>kid's,</u> and he would see the <u>Smith's</u> with their one kid. The <u>Smiths'</u> had <u>cousins'</u> who would come to visit <u>sometime's</u>, and they would always bring <u>present's</u>.

Once the <u>Smiths</u> <u>cousin's</u> brought liver pudding, and another time they brought souse. If you have never had souse, you're in for a real treat. <u>Its</u> a food <u>thats</u> popular in some <u>part's</u> of the United <u>State's</u>.

(<u>Its</u> very hard to inject <u>errors'</u> on purpose. You should try this <u>sometime's</u>.)

Select the correct word.

1. My advise / <u>advice</u> to you is to get out of Dodge as fast as you can. Aunt Ruth is comin', and she means business.

2. I think that's good advise / <u>advice</u>, son. I'll bolt the doors on the saloon and we'll see if Aunt Ruth can get past that.

3. I had a boss once who gave me this advise / <u>advice</u>: If you want to dance, you've got to pay the fiddler.

4. Do you need someone to advice / <u>advise</u> you on how to do this worksheet?

Lesson 43

Review 7

Select the appropriate words.

1. I hope Aunt Ruth **wakes** / awakes up in time to take Binky out for a walk.

2. My favorite dessert / **desert** is the Sahara, though I get thirsty just thinking about it.

3. I was literally / **figuratively** starving to death last night during the show.

4. **All right** / Alright folks, we've got to leave if we're going to see Binky star in Aunt Ruth's latest movie.

5. I like chocolate **a lot** / alot.

6. The only advise / **advice** I can give you is that two elephants in one little apartment might not be a good idea.

7. That's just a **dessert** / desert that **needs to be** / needs eaten.

8. Old MacDonald had a farm with many different kinds of animals, i.e., / **e.g.,** a big cow.

9. Mrs. MacDonald loved living on the farm and reaping the many benefits of country living, **e.g.** / i.e., fresh eggs every morning.

Find the errors in apostrophes in the paragraph below.

Once upon a time, there was an elderly woman named Effie. Now, **Effies** ^{Effie's} favorite food to eat was **macaroni's** ^{macaroni} and cheese. She also liked trying graham **crackers'** ^{crackers} in a bowl of milk at **time's**. ^{times} **Effies** ^{Effie's} aunt was Aunt Ruth, and Aunt **Ruths** ^{Ruth's} favorite thing to do was to take Effie shopping, especially to the hat store. One day they were passing by the fish market, and Aunt Ruth asked Effie if she wanted a salmon. Effie said she loved **salmon's** ^{salmon}, so Aunt Ruth bought her one. Effie put it on her head, and from that day on she never wore any of her other **hats'**. ^{hats}

Lesson 44

Affect, Effect, and Unique

Select the correct word.

1. Is your sleep **affected** / effected when I put my tuba to your ear at night?

2. I've heard that reading grammar books can **affect** / effect your mind in detrimental ways.

3. Do you notice any affect / **effect** when you try to think about lie and lay while standing on your head?

4. I'm not sure how knowing Aunt Ruth will **affect** / effect you, but be assured that there will be some long lasting affects / **effects** from which you will never fully recover.

5. That movie had some very interesting sound affects / **effects**.

6. What do you suppose the affect / **effect** would be if we turned up the guitar amplifier all the way?

7. Caffeine **affects** / effects different people in different ways.

Rewrite the following sentences so they are correct.

8. Sam was thrilled because Aunt Ruth's letter included a very unique postage stamp of a hen on somebody's head.

   Sam was thrilled because Aunt Ruth's letter included a unique postage stamp of a hen on somebody's head.

9. The first time Aunt Ruth thought she was stepping into the time machine, she ended up in the washing machine. The spin cycle effected her for months.

   The first time Aunt Ruth thought she was stepping into the time machine, she ended up in the washing machine. The spin cycle affected her for months.

Lesson 45

Comma Usage I

Fix the comma errors in the following sentences. Add or remove commas where needed.

1. "Hey" said Aunt Ruth "get back here and eat your dinner."
   "Hey," said Aunt Ruth, "get back here and eat your dinner."

2. Kids I need you to eat every carrot tomato and pea on your plate.
   Kids, I need you to eat every carrot, tomato, and pea on your plate.

3. I went to the post office to pick up a package and then to the grocery store to pick up some stomach relief medicine.
   I went to the post office to pick up a package and then to the grocery store to pick up some stomach relief medicine. (No change needed)

4. I went to the hospital to have the doctor remove the fruitcake I had eaten and then I went to the post office to mail the fruitcake back to Aunt Ruth.
   I went to the hospital to have the doctor remove the fruitcake I had eaten, and then I went to the post office to mail the fruitcake back to Aunt Ruth.

5. Aunt Ruth for my birthday gave me twenty-seven cents two aluminum TV dinner trays an expired ticket to Palm Springs and a purebred Guernsey cow.
   Aunt Ruth, for my birthday, gave me twenty-seven cents, two aluminum TV dinner trays, an expired ticket to Palm Springs, and a purebred Guernsey cow.

6. Always one to worry Aunt Ruth the indomitable one rarely overlooks details especially the seemingly insignificant ones.
   Always one to worry, Aunt Ruth, the indomitable one, rarely overlooks details, especially the seemingly insignificant ones.

7. Written by Carl Sandburg the biography of Lincoln that I am reading, is really good.
   Written by Carl Sandburg, the biography of Lincoln that I am reading is really good.

Lesson 46

Comma Usage II

Indicate whether the sentences below correctly use commas. Rewrite the sentences that use commas incorrectly.

1. Y At the football game, Aunt Ruth ordered seven hamburgers, five large fries, three onion rings, and a small diet cola.

2. Y At the basketball game, Aunt Ruth ordered five hot dogs, three large nachos and a bowl of ice cream. (In a list, the comma after the next-to-last item is (though preferred) optional.)

3. N First, I need you, to wash the dishes very carefully.
       First, I need you to wash the dishes very carefully.

4. N Eat every carrot, and pea on your plate.
       Eat every carrot and pea on your plate.

5. N Jeremy the spider is on your shoulder (Jeremy is not a spider).
       Jeremy, the spider is on your shoulder (Jeremy is not a spider).

6. Y Aunt Ruth said, "Say, that's not an elephant."

7. N The elephant said "Say, that's not a great aunt."
       The elephant said, "Say, that's not a great aunt."

8. N The elephant, said "The other night, I shot an aunt in my pajamas."
       The elephant said, "The other night, I shot an aunt in my pajamas."

9. N Aunt Ruth, the adventurous one was off on another escapade.
       Aunt Ruth, the adventurous one, was off on another escapade.

10. Y "I think I need to tell you this," said Aunt Ruth, "and then I'll tell you that."

Lesson 47

Nauseous and Nauseated

Read the following and answer the questions.

Aunt Ruth was nauseous. Which of the following is the best answer?

a.   Aunt Ruth wasn't feeling well.

b.   Aunt Ruth caused me to not feel well.

c.   ✓ It is an ambiguous statement and could mean either (a) or (b).

Which statements below are true, as described in the book?

d.   If something is nauseous, it always makes someone nauseated.

e.   ✓ If something is nauseous, it may make someone nauseated, or it may be nauseated itself.

Led and Lead

Select the correct word in the sentence below.

1. Yesterday, Aunt Ruth lead / **led** a whole herd of lemmings over a cliff.

2. Be careful—Aunt Ruth is carrying around an umbrella made out of **lead** / led.

3. He has successfully lead / **led** armies in the past. I think we can leave him in charge of Little Big Horn.

4. It is not the case that you have to be a world leader in order to contract led / **lead** poisoning.

5. I'm not sure how to get there—you had better **lead** / led the way.

Lesson 48

Phenomena, Criteria, and Data

In the sentences below, select the best choice for each question.

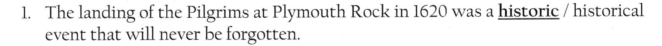

1. The single <u>criterion</u> / criteria for choosing the candidate is based solely on his or her command of English grammar.

2. There are many criterion / <u>criteria</u> we should use when evaluating this decision.

3. The history of weather has included some strange <u>phenomena</u> / phenomenon over the years.

4. The triple play is a most unusual <u>phenomenon</u> / phenomena in baseball.

5. One piece of data / <u>datum</u> suggests that we should be eating grammar crackers for breakfast.

Historic, Historical, Whether, and If

In the sentences below, select the best choice for each question.

1. The landing of the Pilgrims at Plymouth Rock in 1620 was a <u>historic</u> / historical event that will never be forgotten.

2. We have historic / <u>historical</u> records of my grandparents and great grandparents, some of the early settlers in Nebraska.

3. You should call the radio station to determine <u>whether</u> / if it might rain this afternoon.

4. Let me know whether / <u>if</u> you decide to go to the game (I only want to know if your decision is affirmative).

5. Let me know either way if / <u>whether</u> you decide to go to the game.

Lesson 49

Review 8

Select the appropriate words.

1. How does being related to Aunt Ruth **affect** / effect your daily life?

2. Most people think that Aunt Ruth is a **unique** / very unique character.

3. Did you notice any unusual affects / **effects** after dining with Aunt Ruth?

4. Those fumes are **nauseous** / nauseated—they make me feel sick.

5. Jake lead / **led** the expedition up the mountain .

6. Every year there are several **phenomena** / phenomenon surrounding Aunt Ruth that just cannot be explained.

7. The primary criteria / **criterion** for being on Aunt Ruth's good side is simply to not lay an egg on her head.

8. With our metal detector, we were able to find an old wagon wheel (I think belonging to Aunt Ruth's first vehicle) and a few other historic / **historical** artifacts deep in the woods.

9. Try to let me know whether / **if** you are going to come (I only need to know if you do decide to come).

10. Try to let me know **whether** / if you are going to come (let me know either way).

Rewrite the following sentences so they are correct.

11. I ran, and played.
    I ran and played.

12. I ate broccoli a bratwurst, and chocolate.
    I ate broccoli, a bratwurst, and chocolate.

13. "Larry don't forget, to bring home your laundry", said Mrs. Sauerkraut.
    "Larry, don't forget to bring home your laundry," said Mrs. Sauerkraut.

Lesson 50

Comprehensive Review Part 1

Select the appropriate words.

Chapter 1

1. Most people do not realize that Ruth Van Winkle once laid / **lay** down and slept for twenty years.

2. Just lie / **lay** the liver on a shelf in the fridge. Aunt Ruth will pick it up to-morrow.

3. I have lied / **lain** / laid on a water bed.

4. I **laid** / lay the blanket on the water bed.

Chapter 2

5. Hopefully, / **I hope that** she won't forget to take Binky on the ferris wheel.

6. **Hopefully**, / I hope that the farmer planted the seeds in the field.

7. **Hopefully**, / I hope that I went walking without an umbrella.

8. Hopefully, / **I hope that** she remembers to meet me at the right location.

Chapter 3

9. You're acting a small / **little** grumpy this morning.

10. I was a small / **little** upset when I learned Aunt Ruth had borrowed my jet pack.

11. Aunt Ruth is a **little** / small country and a **little** / small rock and roll.

Lesson 51

Comprehensive Review Part 2

Select the appropriate words.

Chapter 4

1. Yes, I am **he** / him.

2. Yes, this is **he** / him.

3. She gave the meatloaf to Hank and **me** / I.

4. Ask not for who / **whom** the bell tolls, but watch out for that falling piano.

Chapter 5

5. **Am** / Are I not the king?

6. **Aren't** / Amn't I the king?

7. You **aren't** / ain't as crazy as Aunt Ruth said you were.

8. You're looking for Aunt Ruth's nephew? That's me / **I**.

Chapter 6

One or more sentences below is incorrect. Rewrite the incorrect sentence(s).

9. Twenty-two baseball cards comprise my collection.
   My collection comprises twenty-two baseball cards.

10. Seventeen chickens and four kids comprise my family.
    My family comprises seventeen chickens and four kids.

11. Aunt Ruth's vocabulary is comprised of many idioms. (Okay)

12. Aunt Ruth's fruitcake comprises all the necessary ingredients with which to build a small brick wall. (Okay)

Lesson 52

Comprehensive Review Part 3

Select the appropriate words.

Chapter 7

1. Can / **May** I have a turn throwing the pie at Aunt Ruth?

2. **Can** / May you leap a tall building in a single bound?

3. Can / **May** I have another bratwurst, please?

4. **Can** / May you play the tuba?

Chapter 8

5. I think Aunt Ruth needs to look into this electric casket warmer idea a little farther / **further**.

6. I have studied Hamlet a little farther / **further** in depth than you have.

7. I think I can throw Aunt Ruth a bit **farther** / **further** than you can. (Either is OK)

8. I think I can throw Aunt Ruth a bit **farther** / **further** than I can throw you. (Either is OK)

Chapter 9

9. You look **as though** / like you just saw Aunt Ruth.

10. Aunt Ruth looks as / **like** Albert Einstein on a bad hair day.

11. I feel **like** / as a blob of strawberry jello this morning.

12. You look **as though** / like you want to say something important.

Lesson 53

Comprehensive Review Part 4

Select the appropriate words.

Chapter 10

1. The tuba which / **that** Aunt Ruth plays is a nice horn.

2. This book, **which** / that is the author's first, is my favorite of all.

3. The elephant **that** / which is in the corner—yes, the one sipping a lemonade—is Aunt Ruth's.

4. The rock band which / **that** Aunt Ruth plays in is too loud for me.

Chapter 11

5. If I was / **were** smarter, I wouldn't have made that mistake.

6. If I **were** / was a professional baseball player, I'd jump for joy.

7. If I **were** / was the king of a small island, I'd eat coconuts every day.

8. If you knew I **was** / were at the game, why did you ask me if I went?

Chapter 12

Circle the examples of verbing or verbizing that you find.

9. The writer has decided to **author** a book.

10. It is our turn to **host** the party.

11. I shall be **breakfasting** a bit earlier than usual, I'm afraid.

12. Any idea what you're going to be **gifting** him for his birthday?

Lesson 54

Comprehensive Review Part 5

Select the appropriate words.

Chapter 13

1. Each person needs to brush **his** / their own teeth.

2. None of us are / **is** exempt from the laws of grammar.

3. Anybody can go get a drink of water if they want / **he wants**.

4. Everybody wishes that **he or she** / they can have an Aunt Ruth.

Chapter 14

5. Do you think you shall / **will** go to the movies tomorrow night?

6. I think he **will** / shall laugh when he hears your story.

7. I think I **will** / **shall** spend the evening reading a book. (Either is OK)

8. It sounds like you **will** / shall go to the store in the morning, right?

Chapter 15

9. Its / **It's** a good thing you are doing this lesson right now!

10. The hair on it's / **its** back was a neon green.

11. **It's** / its it's / **its** own master.

12. **It's** / its a long row to weed.

13. **Its** / It's most amazing attributes are that **it's** / its purple, **it's** / its fuzzy, and **it's** / its crawling up Aunt Ruth's back.

Lesson 55

Comprehensive Review Part 6

Chapter 16

Keeping the parentheses, rewrite and correct the following sentences.

1. Aunt Ruth (the paragon of rational thinking)**,** put her groceries in an aquarium.
   Aunt Ruth (the paragon of rational thinking) put her groceries in an aquarium.

2. Aunt Ruth washed her hair with sauerkraut (her favorite food**.**)
   Aunt Ruth washed her hair with sauerkraut (her favorite food)**.**

3. I need to buy chocolate (my favorite comfort food) some bread, and a cow.
   I need to buy chocolate (my favorite comfort food)**,** some bread, and a cow.

Chapter 17

Select the appropriate words.

4. Aunt Ruth is afraid to go jogging because she looses / <u>loses</u> her way even when she is running in place.

5. My shoelaces are too tight. Could you help me make them lose / <u>loose</u>?

6. Even the best team will <u>lose</u> / loose a game.

Chapter 18

Select the appropriate words.

7. I got an A on my test; the flowers are blooming, and Aunt Ruth is coming over for dinner. Life is <u>good</u> / well!

8. My fingertips are numb. I don't feel good / <u>well</u>.

9. How am I doing? I am doing good / <u>well</u>, thank you.

Lesson 56

Comprehensive Review Part 7

Chapter 19

Circle all the errors with apostrophes you find.

I love these **apostrophe's**^apostrophes. Their tendency to become possessive can be annoying in a way, because **apostrophe's**^apostrophes can tell us that Jeff's car is a purple van, or Kim's chocolate chip **cookie's**^cookies are hidden on top of the fridge. **Theyre**^They're also useful for **contraction's**^contractions, letting us say that your **babys**^baby's due in **moment's**^moments. In general, **theyre**^they're useful. They help us to know that a **dogs'**^dog's best friend is pizza, or that an **elephants**^elephant's trunk isn't something to take lightly but it's great for long **trip's**^trips. **Its**^It's really a great thing, wouldn't you agree? If we asked people, I think most would agree we should keep **apostrophe's**^apostrophes; we just need to be careful how we use them.

Circle the appropriate words in the sentences below.

Chapter 20

1. That movie is **really** / real good.

2. That bad man is real / **really** bad.

3. The real real estate lady is **really** / real pleasant.

4. Real / **Really**, real men eat quiche.

Chapter 21

5. Their / **They're** likely to get upset in airport security if you tell them you are from Mars.

6. **There** / They're is a better way to do this, you know.

7. There / **Their** pumpkin weighs over four hundred pounds!

8. **There** / They're is they're / **their** suitcase that there / **they're** taking with them.

Lesson 57

Comprehensive Review Part 8

Select the appropriate words.

Chapter 22

1. Your / **You're** sitting on my possum.

2. **Yours** / Your's is the one with the purple feathers.

3. **You're** / Your the first one to speak at Aunt Ruth's coronation ceremony.

4. I do believe the tuba that fell out the window is your's / **yours**.

Chapter 23

5. That brown tie does not compliment / **complement** your gray shirt.

6. Please, take another trip in the time machine—it's complementary / **complimentary**.

7. Hand me that paper please. I am writing a letter and need stationary / **stationery**.

Chapter 24

8. **Regardless** / Irregardless, I think you shouldn't have hit her over the head with that fruitcake. I was going to start building a retaining wall in the backyard with it.

9. Irregardless / **Regardless** of who will be there, to whom will you give the hedgehog?

10. **Regardless** / Irregardless of the circumstances, the fact is that Aunt Ruth ate three whole cheesecakes in one sitting.

11. Irregardless / **Regardless** of the fact that Aunt Ruth was dining with the Queen, Aunt Ruth fell asleep in the Queen's comfy chair.

Lesson 58

Comprehensive Review Part 9

Chapter 25

Find the capitalization errors.

<u>the</u> man walked down to the market on a <u>**Fine**</u> <u>**saturday**</u> morning, trying to find something to <u>**Eat**</u>. He was <u>**Extremely**</u> <u>**Hungry**</u> and he bought the first thing he saw, which was five pounds of bratwurst from Bratwurst Unlimited. He was happy with his <u>**Acquisition**</u> and was about to leave, but he saw his friend the <u>**Mayor**</u> and walked over to talk with him. The man greeted the <u>**Mayor**</u>—this was <u>**mayor**</u> Ed, by the way—and the <u>**Mayor**</u> returned the greeting. The mayor then told the man about a new vendor at the market who was selling birds, and they were <u>**Delicious**</u>. <u>**now**</u>, this wasn't just any kind of bird. It was a sea bird. <u>**the**</u> man was sad because he had spent all his <u>**Money**</u>, but the <u>**Mayor**</u> suggested the man selling the birds might be willing to <u>**Trade**</u>. <u>**the**</u> man walked over, introduced himself, and he was delighted to find that the vendor indeed would trade. So the man took a <u>**Tern**</u> for the <u>**Wurst**</u>.

Chapter 26

Find the split infinitives.

"Ah, to seek, to explore, <u>**to bravely venture**</u> where no human has ever ventured before," said the man to himself, as he walked up to the door of Aunt Ruth's apartment. He rang the doorbell and was surprised <u>**to unexpectedly see**</u> the door open in two halves—a top half and a bottom half. The door was split.

"Hello!" said Aunt Ruth, greeting the man. "Sorry for the delay. I was out back, splitting firewood <u>**to cozily burn**</u> in the fireplace. Would you like <u>**to quickly come**</u> in for some ice cream with bananas, chocolate and caramel toppings, whipped cream, and nuts?"

"Oh, you mean a banana split? I'd love <u>**to delightfully have**</u> one!"

Aunt Ruth loved <u>**to graciously entertain**</u> guests in her split level apartment and was sad when the man said he had <u>**to immediately split**</u> upon finishing his dessert. She went to the store to prepare for the next visitor.

Lesson 59

Comprehensive Review Part 10

Chapter 27

Rewrite these sentences containing dangling participles or modifiers.

1. Creamy with rich chocolate, Milton was drooling over the cake.
   Milton was drooling over the cake, creamy with rich chocolate.

2. Weighing over one thousand pounds, Aunt Ruth was impressed with the large pumpkin at the state fair.
   Aunt Ruth was impressed with the large pumpkin, weighing over one thousand pounds, at the state fair.

Chapter 28

Select the appropriate words.

3. I think you should give the meatloaf to **whomever** / whoever you find.

4. George couldn't find the dragon, so he went home to find whomever / **whoever** it was who had told him about it.

5. Come out, come out, whomever / **whoever** you are.

Chapter 29

6. I have swam / **swum** across my bathtub when I was in better shape.

7. I **swam** / swum across the river this morning.

8. Have you ever **bought** / buyed an elevator? It has its ups and downs.

Chapter 30

9. There are **many** / much ways to get tricked by the English language.

10. How **much** / many oatmeal can you eat in one sitting?

Lesson 60

Comprehensive Review Part 11

Chapter 31

Select the appropriate words.

1. Doris, I found the aardvark. It's sitting on the couch, among / **between** you and me.

2. Even with the tension of finding herself alone in a room full of hyenas, Marlene was laughing too because she knew that she was **among** / between friends.

3. **Between** / Among the seven of us, we managed to carry Aunt Ruth home after her unusual accident involving the handkerchief, the feather, and the Ace of Spades.

4. Itchy Jones received his nickname when, on his first parachute jump, he landed in a field **among** / between thousands of poison ivy plants.

Chapter 32

5. The students wanted Aunt Ruth to become the principle / **principal** of the school.

6. Everyone could **accept** / except that the clown had sprayed water on Jimmy Spivey, accept / **except** of course for Mrs. Spivey.

7. The **principal** / principle reason I didn't do well in grade school was because I once accidentally spilled chocolate milk on the **principal's** / principle's tie.

Chapter 33

8. **Wake** / Awake me up when Aunt Ruth is done with her speech.

9. Aunt Ruth collects interesting things, **e.g.** / i.e., TV dinner trays.

10. Aunt Ruth, e.g. / **i.e.**, my great aunt, sure gets a lot of attention these days.

11. I was wokened / **wakened** when Aunt Ruth fell through the ceiling.

Lesson 61

Comprehensive Review Part 12

Chapter 34

Select the appropriate words.

1. Lawrence's lesser known brother, Clarence of Arabia, spent most of his life in search of the perfect chocolate desert / **dessert**.

2. Aunt Ruth, how can we **ensure** / insure that you never vacuum up my dog again?

3. I literally / **figuratively** gained about 2000 pounds at dinner last night.

Chapter 35

4. It's alright / **all right**, Georgette; I ate alot / **a lot** of chocolate mousse too.

5. I think you kids are **all right** / alright.

6. I like Aunt Ruth **a lot** / alot.

Chapter 36

Rewrite these sentences containing dropped infinitives.

7. The grapefruit needs peeled. (The grapefruit needs to be peeled.)

8. The baklava needs harvested. (The baklava needs to be harvested.)

9. Aunt Ruth needs dusted. (Aunt Ruth needs to be dusted.)

10. Binky needs bathed. (Binky needs to be bathed.)

Lesson 62

Comprehensive Review Part 13

Select the appropriate words.

Chapter 37

1. Jacks / <u>**Jack's**</u> birthday wish was to go to the zoo with Aunt Ruth.

2. Aunt Ruths / <u>**Ruth's**</u> lips stuck together after she mistakenly brushed her teeth with super glue.

3. The <u>**Robinsons**</u> / Robinson's aren't home at the moment.

4. The Joneses / <u>**Jones's**</u> houseboat sank when Aunt Ruth leaned too far to one side.

Chapter 38

5. The best advise / <u>**advice**</u> I can give you is to buy all the Aunt Ruth trading cards you can find.

6. I think it's important for kids to advice / <u>**advise**</u> parents on the latest slang.

7. My mom gave me this <u>**advice**</u> / advise: Never be <u>**advised**</u> / adviced by a close relative.

Chapter 39

8. I was <u>**affected**</u> / effected deeply the day I heard on the news that Aunt Ruth won the international hot dog eating contest.

9. Aunt Ruth is a <u>**unique**</u> / very unique individual.

10. What were the affects / <u>**effects**</u> of spending a week on a cruise ship with Aunt Ruth?

11. Read this grammar book and see how it <u>**affects**</u> / effects you.

Lesson 63

Comprehensive Review Part 14

Chapter 39, Comma Usage

Rewrite the sentences below so that they correctly use commas.

1. Aunt Ruth who was sleepy and grumpy reminded me of two of Snow White's friends.
    Aunt Ruth, who was sleepy and grumpy, reminded me of two of Snow White's friends.

2. "Wait", said Aunt Ruth, "where are you going?"
    "Wait," said Aunt Ruth, "where are you going?"

3. I need to go to the post office, and then home.
    I need to go to the post office and then home.

4. Irving from Sleepy Hollow, was terrified of long winter naps.
    Irving, from Sleepy Hollow, was terrified of long winter naps.

5. The Headless Horseman, also from Sleepy Hollow was terrified of Irving.
    The Headless Horseman, also from Sleepy Hollow, was terrified of Irving.

6. "Hey" said the duck "just put it on my bill."
    "Hey," said the duck, "just put it on my bill."

7. Phyllis dreaded her upcoming date, with the Invisible Man as she didn't want to be seen, in public with him.
    Phyllis dreaded her upcoming date with the Invisible Man as she didn't want to be seen, in public with him.

8. Leonardo da Jones, grocer and distant cousin of the famous artist, told the joke that, made Mona Lisa smile.
    Leonardo da Jones, grocer and distant cousin of the famous artist, told the joke that made Mona Lisa smile.

Lesson 64

Comprehensive Review Part 15

Select the appropriate words.

Chapter 40

1. When I'm near you, I feel queasy; you must be **nauseous** / nauseated.

2. I am **nauseous** / nauseating; I feel awful!

Chapter 41

3. Some people would rather be lead / **led**, but Aunt Ruth is a natural leader.

4. Don't eat paint chips; they might contain **lead** / led, which would be harmful to your body.

Chapter 42

5. An interesting phenomena / **phenomenon** about Aunt Ruth is that she never does quite what one expects of her.

6. Some of the most bizarre **phenomena** / phenomenon in the known world involve Aunt Ruth and her various relatives.

7. The chief **criterion** / criteria for selecting Aunt Ruth as president has something to do with her ability to win an arm wrestling contest with the previous president.

Chapter 43

8. In a **historic** / historical moment, Aunt Ruth went back in time to the D-Day invasion and helped the Allied troops in their ultimate victory.

9. **Whether** / If you want ketchup or mustard on your hamburger doesn't really matter; we're having chicken instead.

10. Old family historic / **historical** records indicate that Aunt Ruth consistently improved the grammar of all those around her.